BEYOND THE SMILE
"NOT BROKEN, JUST BRUISED"

CINDY WITTEMAN

© 2024 ALL RIGHTS RESERVED.

Published by She Rises Studios Publishing www.SheRisesStudios.com.

No part of this book may be reproduced or transmitted in any form whatsoever, electronic, or mechanical, including photocopying, recording, or by any informational storage or retrieval system without the expressed written, dated and signed permission from the publisher and author.

LIMITS OF LIABILITY/DISCLAIMER OF WARRANTY:

The author and publisher of this book have used their best efforts in preparing this material. While every attempt has been made to verify the information provided in this book, neither the author nor the publisher assumes any responsibility for any errors, omissions, or inaccuracies.

The author and publisher make no representation or warranties with respect to the accuracy, applicability, or completeness of the contents of this book. They disclaim any warranties (expressed or implied), merchantability, or for any purpose. The author and publisher shall in no event be held liable for any loss or other damages, including but not limited to special, incidental, consequential, or other damages.

ISBN: 978-1-960136-84-8

Table of Contents

Introduction 5
Uncovering the Beginnings 6
Hurdle After Hurdle 10
Forging Ahead Amidst Overwhelming Loss 12
Time to Level Up 18
The Cycle Continued 20
Career Transformation 27
Forgiveness 32
Overcoming Self Sabotage 33
Inspired to give back 39
Taking Action 41
A Life Beyond Limitations 46
The Power is Within YOU! 47
A Journey From Desperation to Gratitude: 51
An Epiphany Emerged 54
Dream Board 56
Turning Point 57
Putting an End to Worry 59
Taking ACTION 61
The Power of Writing: 63

Crafting a Vision Board for Manifestation 65
The Art of Affirmation 67
Tapping into the Potential of Your Subconscious Mind .. 68
Balancing Dreams and Reality 71
The Significance of Emotional Well-being 76
Unveiling Your Purpose 78
The Power of Your WHY 80
Boundary-less Life 82
Impactful Initiatives 83
Personal, Professional, and Relationship Transformation ... 84
Surpassing the Boundaries of Belief 87
Embracing Fear: A Path to Achievement 89
FOUNDATION OF GRATITUDE 96
SHIFTING YOUR MINDSET: A GUIDE 102
ELIMINATING SELF-DOUBT 105
IN CONCLUSION 111
About the Author 114

Introduction

Welcome to the unfiltered journey of my life. In the pages ahead, I'll unveil the real experiences that have shaped me. In a world in which we often admire others, I want to emphasize the imperfections we all carry. Whether scrolling on a screen or flipping through glossy magazines, no one has it all figured out. This book is a testament to the fact that, just like you, I'm navigating life's twists and turns. Through the highs and lows, I invite you to join me, Cindy Witteman, as I share my genuine, imperfect self. This compilation blends my past experiences with fresh insights, showing that if I can carve out this path, so can you. So, let's stop comparing ourselves to others! In today's world of social media, filters, and carefully curated images, it's easy to feel inadequate. But rest assured: No one has it all figured out, and there are countless individuals out there who admire where you are right now. It's essential for each of us to stop idolizing others and recognize the unique power within ourselves. Believe it or not, that power lies within you, waiting to be shared with the world. We all possess our own special talents, so let's ditch the comparison game and look inward to realize our true potential. Join me on this adventure—get ready, because it's time to embrace the beauty of our shared human experience.

Uncovering the Beginnings

Growing up in Texas, my single mom faced the formidable task of raising me amidst financial struggles. Despite the challenges, while our home was not much to brag about, it was a haven of love and was devoid of violence. The hardships were tangible—my mom battled a disability that prevented her from working for most of my childhood. This reality meant that we often found ourselves without the basic necessities that many take for granted.

The financial constraints were palpable; the disability check, child support, and government assistance fell short of covering our bills. One of my less enjoyable childhood memories involved a monthly routine during the time we received paper food stamps (not the Lone Star card used today). My mom would take me to various gas stations to buy a piece of gum for five cents. The teller would then give me 95 cents in change, and I would return the gum to get back the five cents, providing us with $1 in cash. We repeated this process at multiple locations until there was enough money to purchase a carton of cigarettes, leaving little for food by the end of the month. With the remaining funds, I would choose a sack of potatoes. Despite my young age, I already knew that, by month's end, we may lack not only food but also essentials like water, electricity, and propane—often disconnected.

Potatoes were a practical choice as they could be grown for more food, and they didn't require cooking. I could easily slice them and consume them without concern for food-borne illness. I want to be clear that I'm not speaking negatively about my mom; she is the reason I was forced to learn about thinking ahead, understanding cause and effect, and unconditional love. Our struggles thrust me into a world of adult issues at an early age, and the weight of our circumstances made me self-conscious. The lack of resources sometimes manifested in my appearance, leading to bullying about my clothes and unkempt hair.

Owning a vehicle for essential trips, like to the grocery store or doctor's appointments, was a rare luxury for us. I vividly recall moments when our cars were repossessed. One lasting memory is when my mom, during a repossession, insisted on staying in the vehicle, believing they wouldn't take it with her inside. The repo man pleaded, but she refused. He eventually towed the car with her still inside. Approximately an hour later, she walked back to our house, having been let out over a mile away, barefoot and without money, in a time before cell phones. It was a frightening experience for my young mind, fearing she might not ever return. However, despite the trauma, I developed a can-do attitude and a talent for finding innovative solutions to our problems. I learned the importance of earning money and budgeting at a young age. My mom was very crafty, and I would often take some of the items she made out of plastic canvas to school to sell.

Just another one of my early ideas on how to increase our income. I can still recall approaching strangers as a child, inquiring about how they acquired their nice belongings, such as shoes, clothes, cars, and homes. They consistently attributed their success to having an excellent job, fueling my strong desire to secure one as soon as I could, even though I was too young at the time.

In my early school years, I maintained a discreet presence, driven by a deep fear of being ridiculed. I firmly believed I was too slender and awkward, causing me to steer clear of attention-drawing activities like reading aloud or participating in group projects. My family would often joke about my big nose and how I talked too much. I remember when they purchased a t shirt for me that said, "Help, I'm Talking and I Can't Shut Up." This only solidified my inclination to stay in the background, sidestepping the exploration of my complete potential.

In my early teens, though urged by friends to join the school's cheerleading team, my fear of being visible proved insurmountable. Instead, I opted to be the High School Mascot, entertaining the crowd from behind my costume. Few at school realized that I was the one inside the bulldog outfit. As I matured, it became clear that my family's challenges were unique, prompting me to engage strangers in conversations about the stories behind their possessions, fueled by a deep-seated fear of scarcity.

Despite our financial constraints, love remained a constant thread in our lives. Amidst struggles, my mom consistently expressed her love, offering comfort in the face of adversity. Reflecting on those years, I now wish I could share valuable lessons with her about manifesting dreams and overcoming limiting beliefs.

Hurdle After Hurdle

Although I was very young, I mistakenly believed that marriage would be my escape from our hardships and the beginning of a happy life. Therefore, I married the man I thought would give me my happily ever after. My husband had a job, and we had our own vehicle and all the essentials I lacked growing up.

Anticipation and happiness filled the air as we awaited the arrival of our first child. My husband, brimming with excitement, eagerly embraced the prospect of becoming a father. However, the initial revelation of expecting our first child took an unexpected turn when we discovered we were blessed with TWIN boys.

Despite the initial surprise and a slight deviation from our expectations, we wholeheartedly embraced the joy of having two little boys soon to fill our home with laughter and love. However, a little over halfway through the pregnancy, the unforeseen struck as I went into premature labor. Tragically, our hopes and dreams were shattered, and the two precious lives we had been eagerly awaiting did not survive.

Devastation engulfed us, and the entire experience was marked by an overwhelming sense of grief. The medication administered during the distressing ordeal left me in a groggy state, and as I gradually regained consciousness, my memories were hazy at best.

Amidst this emotional turbulence, a nurse entered the room with a seemingly upbeat demeanor, asking about my well-being. In that fragile state, I mustered the strength to express that I felt a bit unwell, but otherwise okay. The nurse, with unwavering enthusiasm, then posed a question that would forever be etched in my memory: "Would you like to see your sons?"

I replied with a resounding YES, a mix of hope and anticipation filling my heart, thinking that, against the odds, perhaps our twins had miraculously survived. The nurse left hastily, only to return with what seemed like an enormous bundle. My initial excitement turned to shock when she placed two lifeless infants in my arms.

The trauma of that moment pierced through me, and even now, 27+ years later, the memory brings tears to my eyes. The stark contrast between the expectation of life and the cruel reality of loss left an indelible mark, shaping a narrative of heartbreak that has endured throughout the passage of time.

Forging Ahead Amidst Overwhelming Loss

We gave ourselves a little time to grieve the loss of our precious boys, Dustin and Stephen. However, we both knew that we wanted to be parents and it wasn't long before we found out we were pregnant again! At the time, my husband worked on a dairy farm, and we were staying in an airstream trailer on the property. I took the test alone and was over the moon when a double pink line appeared. I ran down the gravel path where my husband was driving a tractor and eagerly showed him the positive test. We hugged, and he gave me a tractor ride back to the trailer. The excitement was overwhelming because I still felt responsible for the loss of our sons—at the time it seemed like my body had let all four of us down.

We were thrilled when we received the news that we were having a baby girl. I prayed it wouldn't be a double pregnancy again out of fear of yet another loss. It was discovered that I have something called an incompetent cervix, and that a surgical procedure was necessary to prevent another loss. The pregnancy went well, other than being placed on bed rest for the duration and a couple of premature labor scares. We welcomed our first daughter into the world the following May, and we were both over the moon with excitement when we brought her home from the hospital.

He was a picture-perfect first-time dad, loving and kind. He would hold her for hours and hated leaving for work. Everything seemed to be going smoothly. It was never perfect, but then again, what marriage is? Especially considering my background growing up in a single-parent home, I honestly had no concept of what a healthy marriage was supposed to look like. So, at the time, everything appeared to be going well as far as I could tell.

However, suddenly there was a dramatic shift. I was never able to figure out precisely what happened. It was just like the experts say: It started off gradually with name-calling, pushing, and emotional abuse. Over time he started drinking, and once we were alone, he would just snap! The violence continued to escalate throughout the marriage. As the years passed, we welcomed two more little girls to the family, and as time continued to slip by, I started to realize that this was not going to get better, that I was truly stuck, and it was probably going to be forever…

People often question why I chose to bring more children into such a difficult marriage. In retrospect, the answer is deceptively simple. My husband had a strong desire to have a larger family, and I clung steadfastly to the notion that marriages are meant to endure. In my optimistic naivety, I held onto the belief that by becoming a better homemaker and ensuring our daughters were shielded from harm, we could mold ourselves into the happy family I had always envisioned. I optimistically believed that the man I married could somehow reclaim his kind and considerate nature. Holding on to the hope of providing my daughters with a two-parent home kept me in the marriage for many years.

Following abuse, I found myself compelled to wear a smile and act as if nothing had happened, whether heading to a family function, entertaining guests, or simply masking the pain to shield my children from fear. This experience taught me valuable lessons: how to refrain from talking back, keep thoughts and opinions to myself, stay out of the way, negotiate effectively, and present things in a manner that lessens the risk of triggering my husband's anger. The mantra became to hide, smile, avoid crying, and demonstrate strength. My inner dialogue reinforced the idea that I had chosen this life, created it, and it was my responsibility to make it work to preserve family unity, steering clear of becoming the stigmatized single mom.

The turning point came as I was watching Dr. Phil while folding laundry and I first heard the quote, "It's better to come from a broken home than it is to grow up in one." I immediately acted as if those words were being spoken directly to me. I quickly grabbed a basket of clothes, a bag of diapers, and my daughters, and left. I realized that by avoiding becoming a single mom I was inadvertently dragging my daughters through hell and teaching them that it was okay to allow someone to treat us this way.

So, there I was, 21 years old and running away from a toxic and abusive marriage with my little girls toward something I had feared since childhood: single parenthood. Coming from a single-parent home, I had always promised myself that I would never end up in that situation. I remember thinking, this cannot be happening—not to me, and not to my daughters!

Summoning the strength to step into the car, preparing to break free from the clutches of this challenging reality, the echoes of that distressing voice resounded in my mind. It kept reminding me of those hurtful things I had come to believe about myself—that I was stupid, ugly, just trash, and that nobody wanted me. I had internalized these beliefs for so long, especially since he would constantly reinforce them by saying that without him, I would end up worthless, just like my mom. It was even suggested that I would pass on the same struggles to my daughters that I experienced growing up. It felt like a dark cloud hanging over me, a haunting tune that intensified the emotional pain I desperately wanted to leave behind.

Adding to this burden were warnings that leaving would lead me down a path of being a nobody, dependent on welfare and food stamps, never achieving anything worthwhile. These ominous predictions struck deep chords, particularly because I harbored childhood fears of ending up in poverty. The last thing I wanted was for my daughters and me to face a life of hardship.

Something made me snap back to reality as I strapped my five-month-old into her car seat. I took a deep breath, got into the car, and headed toward a very uncertain future. During that car ride, I vowed to prove to myself that I could get through this, was worth more, and would teach my daughters how to become strong, independent women with heart, ambition, and self-worth.

Initially, I faced a number of challenges on my path to the future. Establishing my own apartment, I lived in secrecy due to the constant threat of abuse. He tracked me down, seized my car—which was in his name—and stopped making the payments, despite having been the primary provider. Fortunately, my father-in-law had co-signed the car loan, which turned out to be a blessing. He took it upon himself to pay off the car, then reached out and suggested that I purchase it from him. We arranged a budget-friendly payment plan, and I successfully paid off the car in full using my tax refund. Acts of kindness from unexpected sources have consistently played a crucial role in my journey toward success.

Due to enduring a traumatic relationship and the pain stemming from my ex-husband's anger issues, I made the challenging decision to keep my last name. This choice was driven by my desire to shield my daughters from associating their last name with negativity. Recognizing that their birth certificates, school papers, and future applications would bear that name, I embarked on a mission to transform it into something they would be proud to carry throughout their lives.

My motivation was clear—I didn't want them to search their name online only to find an inmate status or a criminal record. Instead, I envisioned a name that held value, that was associated with helping others, kindness, and demonstrating that challenges can serve as powerful motivation.

Time to Level Up

Before I knew it, I was juggling two jobs and pursuing further education. Driving my Ford Escort across the city from school to work to babysitters, I'd return home exhausted and tuck the girls into bed, only to repeat the cycle the next day. I knew there was something more for me out there and searched for ways to get off the roller coaster. Influenced by medical dramas like ER, I aimed to become a nurse, thinking it would bring pride to my daughters. I persevered until I had my own place, a car paid in full in my name, and the warm hugs from my daughters after walking the stage at my college graduation.

However, the harsh reality set in—I discovered no satisfaction in nursing. Despite my initial enthusiasm and dedication, the day-to-day responsibilities left me feeling unfulfilled and disconnected. Encountering resistance at every turn was disheartening, with my efforts often yielding little progress. Each shift felt like a battle, a constant struggle between my desire to make a difference and an overwhelming sense of dread. It seemed as though I was investing my heart and soul into a career that didn't resonate with me, merely to meet others' expectations of success. Despite my earnest efforts, I couldn't shake the feeling that I was living someone else's dream, not my own. Consequently, I made the decision to leave nursing and continued working my full-time job at a furniture and electronics store, along with a second job, finally earning enough to meet our basic needs. Being a single mom and lacking financial support for my daughters made this period particularly challenging.

The Cycle Continued

Yet, the narrative didn't take a turn toward a blissful story. I found myself ensnared once more in the cycle of abuse. The subsequent serious relationship unfolded with a man from my workplace. Despite not fitting my usual preferences, he confessed his love for me at a company Christmas party. This revelation caught me off guard, and I promptly dismissed it since I avoid relationships with colleagues and there was absolutely no attraction on my part. However, as time passed, he accepted a promotion and was assigned to a different location, prompting me to reconsider. The motivation behind giving it a chance stemmed from a simple desire—to find someone who could love me and my daughters the way we deserved, as the allure of a seemingly attractive man with a six-pack had proven insufficient.

Since the girls and I were already acquainted with him from work, the introduction was smooth. We got along well, and he proved to be incredibly good with my daughters. I was elated at the prospect of having found a genuinely good man, and his family turned out to be equally amazing and kind to my girls. For close to a year, everything seemed idyllic. He exhibited kindness, generosity, and helpfulness, and we engaged in activities together as if we were a genuine family.

Once again, however, life took a sharp turn. It happened during what was supposed to be a fun date night, but it quickly turned into a nightmare. As the evening progressed, my partner indulged in one drink too many, and I sensed trouble brewing beneath the surface. There was something in his eyes, a glint of volatility that sent shivers down my spine. Instinctively, I knew we had to leave before things escalated further.

But my attempt to diffuse the situation only fueled his rage. In a terrifying moment on the drive home, he lashed out, grabbing me violently and slamming my head against the steering wheel of the truck. His demand for me to declare my love felt like a cruel joke, especially since I had been holding back those words until I was absolutely sure.

As we veered off the road into an empty field, fear gripped me like never before. He commanded I get out and run for my life. I pleaded, my voice trembling with desperation, fully aware of the danger that awaited me outside the safety of the truck. In that moment, survival instincts kicked in, learned during years of navigating my previous abusive marriage.

My mind raced with thoughts of my daughters, imagining the impact of my potential demise on their innocent lives. The fear was amplified by the realization that no one would suspect him of any wrongdoing. After all, he had always been the epitome of kindness and charm.

In that moment, I grappled with the reality of my situation, forced once again to navigate the murky waters of abuse and manipulation. But amidst the chaos, one thought remained clear: my unwavering determination to survive, not just for myself, but for the sake of my daughters and the promise of a better tomorrow.

As I sat there, terrified, I knew I had to find a way to deescalate the situation and protect myself from harm. Drawing upon every ounce of strength and resilience within me, I resorted to the negotiation skills I had learned during my previous abusive relationship. With a shaky voice, I recited whatever words I thought would buy me precious moments of safety.

But even as I played along, thoughts raced through my mind. What if this was the end? What if I never made it back to my daughters, to the life I had fought so hard to build? Those possibilities felt heavy, almost too much to bear.

Eventually, after my pleading, he agreed to drive me back home. When we pulled into the driveway, I noticed my brother's car parked there. He had been looking after my sleeping daughters. As we arrived, he grabbed my arm firmly, warning me to stay quiet and go straight to my room. I quickly unlocked the front door and dashed to the room my brother was in, seeking help. My brother, startled from sleep, hastily put on some shorts as I desperately held the door shut. He was disoriented and half-awake, trying to comprehend the situation. Suddenly, without any warning, the man burst into the room and chased my brother out of the house, locking the door behind him. Now, my daughters and I were left alone with this irrational, violent, and intoxicated man.

The abuse escalated; he pulled my hair and spit in my face several times. I was gripped by terror, fearing that he might wake my sleeping girls and, worse, possibly harm them. Considering his ability to pretend to be a loving and caring man for all those months, the extent of his potential actions remained uncertain. Fortunately, my brother happened to have his keys and cellphone in his pocket. Without hesitation, he dialed my dad. With some encouragement, my brother cautiously unlocked the door and handed the phone to the man. My dad, composed and strategic, managed to persuade him to calm down and leave for the night.

Despite the intensity of the situation, my daughters remained sound asleep, unaware of the turmoil that had unfolded. Ending the relationship was a choice I made instinctively, without any hesitation. Reflecting on my past experiences with abuse, I recognized that it wasn't an isolated incident. Forgiving would only perpetuate the cycle, allowing the abuse to escalate and become more severe over time.

Believing it was a thing of the past was a complete misconception. He began a relentless pattern of calling and stalking me. On one particularly alarming night, he bombarded me with calls and voicemails, which I refused to answer. Undeterred, he invaded my house with a gun, shattering the mirror on the large dresser in my room. I was not home when this frightening incident unfolded. I remember receiving a frantic call from my brother, who, along with my daughters, had been jolted awake by the shattering sound of the mirror.

Rushing to my minivan to hurry home, I discovered that he had ruthlessly slashed all four of my vehicle tires in the sidewall, effectively preventing my return. Fortunately, a friend was generous enough to drive me home, a time before ride-sharing services were available. By the time I reached home, he had fled the scene, leaving my brother and daughters unharmed. The police arrived and retrieved a gun he had left on my bed. He strategically did this, aware that I lacked the financial means to replace the slashed tires. Thankfully, his parents stepped in and covered the cost of replacement. I shudder to think about what would have happened had it not been for their assistance.

The following incident proved to be even more terrifying. It happened while I was getting ready for work, with my daughters fast asleep. The sound of forceful pounding on the door, accompanied by screams from the front yard, sent a wave of deep-seated fear coursing through my gut. I rushed to my daughter's room and witnessed him brandishing a firearm in the yard. Filled with panic, I quickly pulled my daughter, who was closest to the window, off the bed, shielding her from the potential gunfire.

As I dialed 911, he returned to his truck, momentarily giving the impression that he would leave. However, my assumption proved wrong once again. He reversed his truck and began smashing it into my vehicle, pushing it through the garage door, striking it repeatedly before backing up and driving away. It wasn't until the police arrived that I realized he had slashed all four of my brand-new tires in the sidewall once again and carved an offensive message on the hood of the family minivan. Panicked, I reached out to his parents, and once more, they bore the entire expense of the inflicted damage. In a generous gesture, they even lent me their car, enabling me to commute to work while the repairs were underway. At that time, with only liability car insurance, their assistance prevented me from facing a considerable financial setback. Despite enduring pain, abuse, and loss, it's acts of kindness like this that renew my faith in the inherent goodness of the world.

After a series of alarming incidents, he was eventually apprehended and faced legal consequences for his crimes. I found myself once again having to start anew, rebuilding a life for my daughters and me, despite my deep-seated longing for marriage and a two-parent household, facing yet another setback.

As I closed the door on that frightening chapter, a daunting realization dawned upon me—there was still a significant hurdle to overcome. This hurdle wasn't external but rather internal, a battle with my own fears of abuse and failure. In the chapters that follow, you'll witness my journey as I employ creative strategies to conquer self-sabotage, striving to elevate myself and bring to life the dreams I've envisioned.

Career Transformation

Filled with excitement, I embraced the opportunity of landing a managerial position at my corporate job. This role demanded a minimum of 50 hours per week but offered a significant pay raise and the promise of consolidating my two jobs into one. Initially, everything seemed to fall into place—I secured a comfortable three-bedroom townhouse for my daughters and me, and I also took on the responsibility of caring for my mom, who faced mobility challenges due to her disability. However, as the demands of the new job intensified, I began to notice a widening gap between me and my daughters. My father, noticing this growing divide, candidly pointed out that continuing down this path would mean my daughters growing up with a mother they hardly knew. His words struck a chord within me and prompted a moment of deep reflection.

Together with my father, we devised a plan to address this imbalance. I made the decision to spread out my tax refund over the year and supplement my income by selling plasma twice a week, opting for an unconventional approach to financial stability. Despite initially taking a significant pay cut, this strategy enabled me to meet our basic needs as I transitioned into the legal field. The allure of retirement benefits, holidays off, and a manageable 40-hour workweek

Monday through Friday, which would afford me ample time to spend with my daughters, made the switch all the more appealing.

Motivated by the wisdom imparted by my father, I embraced the challenges of the legal profession with determination. Despite the financial sacrifices, I believed that within a year, I could secure a promotion and make the overall plan work.

Opting to sell plasma seemed like an ideal solution, offering me an additional $300 a month. However, my petite, 106-pound frame didn't respond well to the plan. I vividly recall nearly passing out multiple times during plasma extraction. To avoid that worst-case scenario, I had to devise my own personal tactics. Prior to entering the donation center, I established a routine of grabbing a quick bite in the parking lot, usually indulging in Whataburger French fries. They were affordable, and conveniently, there was a Whataburger located in the same parking lot as the plasma center. It became my routine, ensuring that I wouldn't faint during the extraction process. The thought of being barred from donating due to a health issue was terrifying, especially since I relied heavily on that additional income. So, taking this precaution became essential for me to secure the extra money.

The aftermath of these sessions was challenging. Arriving home in a dazed state, I would gather the energy to prepare dinner while lying on the kitchen floor. Stirring whatever was cooking, I'd then rest on the floor, waiting for my strength to resurface before continuing with the cooking process. Despite the difficulties, my guiding mantra was, "If it's to be, it's up to me." This challenging period tested my resilience, emphasizing the determination required to navigate through tough times.

Looking back, the gratitude I feel toward my father for offering such invaluable advice is profound. This choice to accept the position in the legal field not only illuminated a path to financial stability but also set the stage for a transformative journey in my professional life. Securing three new positions within the inaugural year of my career journey was a testament to my sheer determination, and the real turning point arrived at the 8-month mark when a significant pay increase granted me some much-needed breathing room. Despite this progress, I continued selling plasma to maintain a semblance of financial stability and provide my daughters with a unique experience—dining at restaurants.

Despite tight finances, I transformed our dining experiences into exciting outings for my daughters. I presented them with the option of either appetizers or dessert at restaurants, concealing the fact that it was due to budget constraints. If they chose appetizers, we'd dine out before I prepared dinner at home. On dessert nights, I'd cook dinner first, and then we'd head out for a sweet treat. Seeing their joy, especially during trips to fancier places like Chili's, brought me immense satisfaction and pride. These moments were more than just meals; they represented a fulfillment of the experiences I'd longed for when I was growing up. From the beginning, I made it a tradition for us to gather at the dinner table without distractions. The ritual of sharing the highlights of our day or expressing gratitude during dinner has endured and continues to this day. Maintaining our family connection is crucial to me, especially amid the chaos and challenges we were navigating.

Beyond dining out, I took pride in being able to afford name-brand shoes for my daughters, particularly Sketchers, despite their requests for Nike shoes, which were financially out of reach at the time. This marked a significant departure from the hand-me-downs that characterized my own childhood. However, as my daughters grew older, I learned that they had faced bullying for wearing those shoes. Years later, when I found out about the bullying, it hit me hard. I felt awful because I had thought I was doing something positive for my daughters, only to learn that it had actually contributed to their struggles.

The journey of providing for my daughters not only reflected financial progress but also unearthed the complexities of navigating societal expectations and budget constraints.

Throughout this challenging journey, one critical aspect was noticeably absent: consideration for my own desires. My life was centered around a perpetual struggle for survival, existing in fight, flight, or survival mode. I dedicated my efforts to impressing my father and daughters, solely focused on getting through each day. The result was a life lived on autopilot, lacking passion and genuine fulfillment. I frequently engaged in harsh self-dialogue, criticizing myself for perceived inadequacies and stagnation in both personal and professional aspects. My attempts at self-improvement were hindered by self-sabotage, following a path dictated by external expectations rather than pursuing what truly resonated with me. This pattern extended to my relationships, where I often tried to reshape others to fit into my life instead of seeking individuals who naturally complemented my journey.

Forgiveness

The healing journey extended well beyond the time it took for the physical bumps and bruises to fade. Eventually, I made the conscious decision to forgive, and to this day, I harbor no grudges. Fear and anger have no place in my life now; there's neither time nor space for them. Those who have created struggles in my past no longer wield any power over me or my life, and I opt to gaze forward, not into the rearview mirror, though those times were immensely challenging. I believe forgiveness is a choice we all possess, enabling us to let go of past memories that might otherwise hinder our progress. The decision was straightforward, and I continue to learn and grow as a woman as life moves forward.

Overcoming Self Sabotage

In the unfolding chapters of my life story, I reveal an enduring struggle against self-sabotage, a battle rooted in my childhood and marked by persistent fears and a lingering sense of inadequacy. This internal conflict originated from the challenging circumstances of my upbringing, where financial limitations and a fear of judgment shaped my inclination to avoid the spotlight and opportunities for personal growth. Despite these hurdles, I navigated life's challenges with resilience and determination, striving to overcome the barriers that hold me back and to embrace the path toward self-discovery and fulfillment.

In my thirties, I had a profound realization about how my own limiting beliefs and negative thoughts were holding me back from happiness and growth. This awakening sparked a journey of self-discovery and transformation. I actively challenged my negative thought patterns, set ambitious goals, and began working tirelessly to create a life that truly fulfilled me. This journey was about more than just achieving external success; it was about confronting my deepest fears and insecurities, pushing myself beyond my comfort zone, and seizing every opportunity I could for personal and professional growth.

By altering my mindset and confronting my fears, I actively immersed myself in life, participating in events, advancing my career, and cultivating healthier relationships. I came to realize that the power to change had been within me all along. In the previous section, I touched upon two detrimental relationships, yet there were numerous other unhealthy ones. Recognizing that the common denominator in these relationships was ME became a pivotal realization.

I found myself repeatedly entering into relationships where red flags were glaringly evident, yet I justified and excused the concerning behavior. For instance, I convinced myself that someone's abusive tendencies stemmed from childhood abandonment and believed that having children would somehow mend the broken pieces. In another case, I dismissed a partner's constant drinking as harmless, only to later witness its negative impact on the relationship. The underlying pattern was not to point fingers but to acknowledge my tendency to choose partners with the intent to "fix" them.

My misguided belief that I could help these individuals overcome their issues and transform into healthier partners was a major flaw. Instead of investing time in others, I should have focused on self-reflection and addressing the reasons behind my own behaviors. This transformative realization empowered me to find my voice, break free from negative cycles, support meaningful causes, and forge a path to contributing positively to society.

By highlighting the importance of shifting our perspectives and beliefs to reach our true potential and live a fulfilling life, through perseverance and self-awareness, I discovered the strength within myself to triumph over fear and pursue my dreams.

My fears were rooted in past experiences, particularly my tendency to shy away from the spotlight due to insecurities about my appearance, upbringing, and financial instability. These early struggles molded my inclination to hide my potential and avoid taking risks.

It took me years to truly understand and appreciate myself. When I felt ready, I listened to the Audible version of *Think and Grow Rich* by Napoleon Hill. While listening, I realized that I deserved love, kindness, and respect, and that I was destined for more than being a victim. In 2014, a significant shift occurred as I stepped into my power, embracing a life filled with purpose, giving back, and helping others. It wasn't instant perfection, and challenges persisted. There are moments when life gets me down and fear reappears, and it's unsettling. However, now I've learned to take charge of those thoughts, acknowledging the temporary nature of these feelings, which helps me persevere.

Occasionally, feelings of unworthiness and imposter syndrome creep in, becoming significant stressors. Even on my worst days, I consistently show up, offering a smile and a cheerful greeting to all. It's crucial to emphasize that persisting through the good, bad, and ugly isn't fake. According to a study published by the Mayo Clinic on April

23, 2019 (Michelle Graff-Radford), there's scientific evidence to show that laughter decreases stress, improves mood, and enhances resilience. Smiling or laughing releases chemicals that boost mood and mental health, providing various benefits such as pain relief, improved mood, decreased depression and anxiety, strengthened social connections, reduced tension and cortisol, improved immune system, and increased resilience.

Therefore, anyone who suggests that smiling or laughing through tough days is fake is mistaken. It's a genuine effort not only to uplift one's mood but also to positively impact others.

Realizing that I held the reins to alter the narrative and silence the persistent negative self-talk was a revelation—a personal aspect I could actively improve. Historically, I often perceived my life as heading in an unfavorable direction, attributing it to external factors. However, a fundamental truth emerged: You can't change other people. The moment I authentically grasped the influence I wielded, making the shift became remarkably straightforward. Here are some steps I took to boost my confidence and conquer my ingrained self-sabotaging tendencies:

1. Self-Reflection: Begin by understanding and acknowledging your thoughts and behaviors. Take time for self-reflection to identify patterns of negative self-talk or actions that contribute to self-

sabotage. Be honest with yourself about the areas in which you lack confidence and the situations triggering self-destructive behavior.

2. Setting Realistic Goals: Break down larger objectives into smaller, achievable goals. Success in accomplishing these smaller tasks will gradually build confidence. Celebrate your victories, no matter how minor, and use them as stepping stones toward bigger objectives. This approach helps to create a positive momentum that counteracts self-sabotaging tendencies.

3. Positive Affirmations and Visualization: Develop a repertoire of positive affirmations to challenge and replace negative thoughts. Visualize yourself succeeding and achieving your goals. Regularly affirm your capabilities and visualize the positive outcomes you desire. This practice helps to rewire your mindset, fostering a more optimistic and self-assured outlook.

Upon overcoming fear, self-limiting beliefs, and self-sabotage, my life underwent a rapid transformation. Liberated from these constraints, I began journaling and contemplating my desires. The subsequent developments were almost surreal.

A helpful trick I employed involved wearing a basic rubber band on my wrist and giving it a snap whenever I noticed a negative thought creeping in. While this method might not suit everyone, I can attest that it significantly accelerated the training of my brain, swiftly redirecting it toward more positive thoughts.

Inspired to give back

During my challenging days as a single parent, the desire to give back and support others in similar situations always burned within me. Initially, I aimed to establish a nonprofit focused on childcare, but a poll revealed a lack of enthusiasm, fueled by the misconception that government assistance adequately covered this area. Despite the availability of programs, we faced limitations such as funding constraints, lengthy waitlists, and complicated qualification processes.

Though disheartened by the poll results, I recognized that no nonprofit could thrive without community support. Despite my initial vision, I had to pivot and identify another crucial need for assisting single parents. After months of contemplation, a breakthrough occurred during dinner with my then-fiancé, now husband. The idea struck me suddenly, and I stood up, declaring my intention to give away cars to single parents in need. However, my husband, an attorney, immediately voiced concerns about potential liability issues, urging me to reconsider.

Unfazed, I turned to our waitress for advice, and to my surprise, she too had faced the challenges of single parenthood and unreliable transportation. She recounted her family's struggles, including waiting for public transportation in the rain and other hardships. While she suggested a more modest solution, such as offering Uber or Lyft vouchers, I realized that this would only address the issue temporarily. The vouchers would eventually run out, leaving single parents to grapple with transportation challenges week after week without a lasting solution. While many nonprofits provide essential items like food, clothing, diapers, and formula, offering crucial support, I envisioned creating a nonprofit that would empower single parents with a sustainable solution. Instead of a temporary fix, I aimed to provide reliable vehicles that would enable single parents to secure higher-paying jobs or pursue higher education, ultimately increasing their income and offering a long-term solution.

Taking Action

Taking the leap to launch a nonprofit that focused on aiding single-parent households was both exhilarating and nerve-wracking for me. Amidst the excitement of pursuing a cause close to my heart, I couldn't shake the persistent doubts creeping into my mind. I questioned my own capabilities and wondered if I could truly make a meaningful impact. The fear of failure loomed large, but deep down, I was determined to push through and make a difference, no matter how daunting the journey ahead seemed.

Upon recognizing the pressing need for an organization focused on single parents and supported by data highlighting the prevalence of single-parent homes, I took immediate action. Within 24 hours of conceptualizing the idea, I began crafting a plan and building the organization's website, understanding that delaying action would only fuel my fears and limiting beliefs.

In the early stages of this remarkable journey, just weeks after the idea had been sparked in my mind, I took the plunge by organizing the first car giveaway. It was a momentous occasion that filled me with a mix of excitement and nervousness. Choosing the first recipient, John, was very personal for me. His story resonated deeply—a resilient single dad who had faced unimaginable tragedy. Losing his wife in a devastating drunk driving accident, he had also endured the loss of his leg. Despite these immense challenges, he never gave up. His unwavering strength and determination to provide for his children against all odds left a profound impression on me.

After selecting John as the deserving recipient, I embarked on the task of finding the perfect vehicle. Putting my own funds into it, I carefully chose an SUV that I believed would cater to his children's needs and accommodate his physical limitations. As the date for the giveaway approached, set for April 1st, the anticipation and excitement grew. The event attracted media attention, adding to the buzz surrounding it. I remember the drive to the event vividly, rain pouring down, when John called, half in jest, questioning if it was all an elaborate April Fool's joke. It was then that I realized the unintended significance of the date, adding a touch of serendipity to the occasion.

The giveaway unfolded beautifully, and the joy on John's and his family's faces remains etched in my memory. April 1st, 2017, is a day I will forever remember. During challenging times, I draw on this memory to remind myself that my purpose transcends any struggle or self-doubt. Assuring John that it was no joke, I gave him the keys to his new vehicle that day.

With unwavering support from a dedicated board of directors and volunteers, our impact continues to expand.

However, persistent challenges like self-sabotage and a fear of public speaking demand ongoing attention from my inner critic.

Confronting my fear of public speaking became imperative as I assumed the role of representing the organization. Transitioning from a background role to the forefront proved daunting, yet I persevered, acknowledging that I was my harshest critic. Over time, my confidence grew, and I embraced the opportunity to advocate for our cause. I sought mentorship and gradually honed my skills. Each presentation was a chance to connect with others and share our mission, and with each step forward, I felt more empowered to make a difference. Despite my progress, I still grapple with a fear of public speaking to this day, but I refuse to let it hold me back from advocating for what I believe in.

I'd like to recount another significant moment that truly exemplifies the ripple effect of the organization I founded. In 2020, through a partnership, we had the opportunity to provide another single parent with the gift of transportation. Our recipient, La-Tieka, immediately joined our board of directors with the mission to help the organization grow. She graduated from college and swiftly ascended the ranks of the nonprofit to become the Vice President of Philanthropy. In a crucial moment in 2023, she made a significant announcement: She had bought a vehicle for herself and wished to donate the one she had received from the nonprofit back to the organization, to benefit another single-parent household. This full-circle moment still brings tears to my eyes as I reflect on the tremendous act of selflessness and kindness she displayed. It was truly inspiring to witness La-Tieka hand over the keys to the new recipient and deliver a heartfelt speech expressing how much the vehicle had helped her, and her hopes that it would do the same for the new recipient.

As we mark seven years of Driving Single Parents, I find myself reflecting on the profound impact of our journey. It's been a rollercoaster ride of challenges and triumphs, but every step of the way has been worth it. From humble beginnings to where we stand today, the growth and evolution of our nonprofit have been nothing short of extraordinary.

Our journey has been fueled by the unwavering dedication of our board of directors, whose commitment to our cause knows no bounds. Their tireless efforts and selfless contributions have been the driving force behind our success, and I am endlessly grateful for their support.

Looking back, I can't help but be humbled by the families whose lives we've touched. Each story, each smile, each moment of gratitude serves as a testament to the impact we've had and the difference we've made. It's a reminder of why we do what we do and a source of inspiration to keep pushing forward, no matter the obstacles we may face.

As we continue to grow and expand our reach, I'm filled with a sense of optimism and excitement for the future. There's still so much work to be done and so many lives to touch, and I'm more determined than ever to make a difference. With the support of our dedicated team and the unwavering resilience of the families we serve, I have no doubt that we'll continue to create positive change and build a brighter future for single-parent households.

A Life Beyond Limitations

In this section, I'll share with you the profound impact that learning how to effectively manifest has had on my life. I'll take you on a journey through the struggles I've faced and the successes I've achieved since unlocking the power within me through manifesting and gratitude. Life often throws us challenges that can feel insurmountable, leaving us feeling trapped in circumstances beyond our control. However, my journey challenges this notion by showcasing how I've used the power of my mind to break free from limitations and create a life of abundance. This narrative invites you to step into a world where manifesting, gratitude, and purpose converge to pave the way for a truly transformative experience.

The Power is Within YOU!

Starting my journey of manifestation has shown me that it's not just wishful thinking. It's about tapping into the incredible power of my mind and realizing that the only limits are the ones I create for myself.

Throughout my life's journey, I've often felt trapped by external circumstances, like I was living within invisible walls. But one day, I had a powerful realization: My own mind was both the jailer and the captive. It dawned on me that the key to freedom was right there, hidden in plain sight. I had unknowingly built walls with my own thoughts, keeping myself confined.

Now, having seized that elusive key, I am driven by a determination to guide YOU in unlocking your own prison door. My aim is to empower you to stride confidently into a life brimming with untapped potential and countless possibilities. The journey toward manifestation is not merely a personal revelation but a shared voyage toward self-discovery and the realization that the mind, when harnessed effectively, can be a powerful force for transformation.

A Glimmer of Hope:

As life unfolded, it became apparent that my persistent feelings of scarcity and anxiety were acting as barriers to embracing abundance. A pivotal moment occurred when I stumbled upon a film and book featured on the Oprah Winfrey show titled *The Secret*, by Rhonda Byrne. Initially deeming it absurd, I dismissed the idea and considered its teachings pure nonsense.

Fast forward to 2013, and I found myself grappling with the challenge of improving my circumstances. Faced with a recurring cycle of difficulties despite my efforts, I reached a breaking point. Out of desperation, I decided to give *The Secret* a chance. As a single mother selling plasma twice a week to make ends meet, I embraced the teachings against the backdrop of financial struggle and the need to provide for my daughters.

As I delved deeper into the concept of manifestation, I found myself drawing comparisons to the unseen yet tangible forces of nature, such as electricity and gravity. While these forces are invisible to the naked eye, we can perceive their effects in our daily lives. For instance, we experience the shock of electricity when we touch a live wire, and we witness gravity's influence as objects fall to the ground.

Contemplating these parallels, I began to wonder if manifestation operates based on a similar principle—tapping into an invisible yet potent force that shapes our reality based on our thoughts and intentions. Just as we can harness electricity by plugging into an outlet, perhaps we can tap into this hidden energy field by aligning our thoughts and desires with our actions. This alignment may set in motion a series of events that bring our goals and aspirations to fruition, even if we don't fully grasp the mechanics behind it.

Eager to put the principles of manifestation into practice, I wholeheartedly embraced the teachings outlined in *The Secret*. I embarked on a journey of experimentation, implementing various techniques to manifest my desires. I meticulously wrote blank checks to myself, infusing them with the abundance I wished to attract. I boldly embellished my bank statement with extra zeros, symbolizing the wealth I envisioned. Embracing the power of gratitude, I carried a special rock as a reminder to appreciate the blessings in my life.

In moments of quiet reflection, I vividly visualized myself behind the wheel of my dream car, feeling the exhilaration of driving it with ease and joy. To solidify my intentions, I meticulously crafted a vision board adorned with images that represented my deepest desires and aspirations. Each image served as inspiration, guiding me toward the manifestation of my dreams.

Not so STRAIGHTFORWARD!

Navigating through this journey proved to be a complex challenge, demanding my unwavering commitment and perseverance. Investing months in these manifestation techniques, I poured my heart and soul into the endeavor with unwavering determination. Unfortunately, despite my dedicated efforts, changes in my life remained elusive, leaving me grappling with frustration and harsh self-criticism. Disheartened by what felt like a futile pursuit, I succumbed to irritation, condemning myself for what I perceived as wasted time.

In my moment of frustration, I tossed aside the tools of my manifestation journey. I ripped up the blank check, tore apart the vision board, and hurled the gratitude rock into the peaceful waters of a nearby pond. Then, like a storm brewing, a flood of challenges surged into my life—bills piled higher, my income stalled, and troubles loomed ahead. It felt like everything spiraled into chaos the moment I gave up on manifesting.

A Journey From Desperation to Gratitude:

Yet the pivotal moment unfolded in late 2013. Fueled by desperation, I turned to the Audible versions of *Think and Grow Rich* and *The Secret*, listening with a renewed sense of determination. Committing to instigating change, my New Year's resolution for 2014 centered on embracing the teachings of these materials with a fresh perspective. Rather than pursuing a radical transformation of my entire reality, I aimed to shift my mindset toward positivity. Gratitude for existing blessings, self-compassion, and articulating aspirations became the new pillars I aspired to build upon. This marked a juncture where introspection prompted me to write down my thoughts, hopes, and dreams—an uncharted endeavor. While outlining others' desires came easily, my own felt elusive. To bridge this gap, I directed my energy into gratitude, acknowledging even the seemingly modest aspects of my life.

Engaging in consistent writing sessions became a captivating journey, where the magic of self-expression unfolded night after night. As I allowed my thoughts to flow effortlessly onto paper, they took form, crystallizing into concrete goals and aspirations. As I continued writing each evening, the fog surrounding my dreams started to clear.

This nightly ritual not only shaped my evenings but also transformed the way I approached mornings. Gratitude, once confined to mere acknowledgment, evolved into a deliberate morning practice. The act of expressing thanks for even the seemingly modest aspects of my life became a grounding and affirming ritual.

Each evening, as I faithfully continued these practices, a noticeable transformation began to stir within me. With each stroke of the pen, the haze that once clouded my thoughts began to dissipate. Despite the absence of tangible changes in my external environment, an inner shift took place—an emergence of newfound hope and self-assurance.

This transformation went beyond material possessions. It was a profound alteration in perspective and mindset—a deepening sense of clarity and purpose. Through the simple acts of gratitude and articulating my aspirations, I found strength and resilience building within me.

Every word penned became a thread in the fabric of my evolving narrative—a story of empowerment and determination. As I continued to write, I felt empowered to confront life's challenges with renewed confidence and optimism.

My internal conversation underwent a transformation from self-criticism to empowerment, allowing me to acknowledge achievements such as owning a custom-built four-bedroom house, holding a fulfilling job with benefits, and displaying the strength to raise four children independently. The realization struck me—these accomplishments had always been present, they were just obscured by my previous inability to recognize and celebrate them. This shift in perspective set off a chain reaction of change. My career experienced a surge, friendships deepened, and even my dating life underwent a remarkable transformation. I relinquished the habit of settling for attractive yet flawed partners, choosing instead to prioritize my own desires.

An Epiphany Emerged

In 2021, the profound loss of my mom to COVID-19 added another layer of sorrow to our already challenging narrative, aligning with a pivotal moment in my life. Departing at 61, she had endured earlier years marked by pain and heartbreak.

Contemplating life's fragility, I recognized how, for years, I had confined myself to social norms, concealing my true self and feeling inadequate. The realization that time is the greatest gift emerged prominently, prompting me to cherish not only what I possessed but also the time left for genuine joy and fulfillment. This motivated me to bid farewell to self-sabotage and playing small, expressing gratitude for the valuable lessons my mom imparted during her time on earth.

Since I was young, I've been on a quest for a better life, striving to break free from the shadows of our past. Along the way, I unintentionally drifted from truly understanding my mom's journey. Still, her unwavering love continues to fuel me as I navigate life and parenthood, carrying forward the resilience she embedded in me.

By sharing my story, I hope to shed light on the common struggle with self-doubt and limiting beliefs. We all face these hurdles, but with grit and the courage to confront our fears, we can achieve remarkable breakthroughs. By embracing our potential and trusting in ourselves, we can break free from self-imposed barriers and leave a lasting mark on the world.

Realizing that I hold the reins to my own destiny, my life's narrative isn't dictated by external forces anymore. It's like a blank canvas eagerly awaiting my personal touch. As the fog of uncertainty clears, my future appears radiant, brimming with boundless opportunities.

A pivotal decision to alter my perspective demonstrates the extent of the control I have over my life. It wasn't merely about thinking differently; it was comprehending that I could mold my experiences and determine the trajectory of my life. Understanding the influence of my choices became a guiding light, leading me toward self-discovery and a sense of empowerment.

With this newfound awareness, I recognized the significance of each choice and the impact of shifting my perspective. The metaphorical pen, symbolizing my control, transformed into a tool for crafting a narrative not solely about challenges and successes but also about strength, growth, and an unwavering belief in limitless potential.

Dream Board

Setting out on my journey of self-improvement, I took the plunge and crafted a brand new dream board—a visual representation of my deepest desires. Carefully selecting images, I adorned the board with scenes depicting travel adventures, robust health, financial stability, and thrilling new ventures. Each picture held significance, reflecting the vibrant life I aimed to create.

In the quiet moments of each day, I dedicated time to gazing upon this personalized collage. As my eyes wandered, my mind embarked on a visual journey through scenes symbolizing the potential I envisioned for my future. This ritual became more than observation; it became a bridge connecting my dreams to reality.

Beyond serving as inspiration, the dream board sparked introspection. It guided me to contemplate actionable steps toward realizing my aspirations. No longer limited to daydreaming, I found the drive to actively shape my future.

The dream board evolved into a symbolic compass, pointing me toward my passions. Its visual cues motivated me to turn aspirations into tangible progress. Ultimately, it became a dynamic tool, fueling my journey of self-discovery and encouraging proactive pursuit of the life I desired.

Turning Point

While confronting my personal financial challenges, navigating family hardships, and grappling with the intricacies of single parenthood, I came to a profound understanding: Abundance transcends mere wealth accumulation. It's about maximizing the potential of the resources we possess, leveraging them to create positive change and support those in need. This pivotal realization prompted a significant shift in my mindset, leading me to redirect my efforts from solely pursuing financial gain to actively seeking opportunities to give back and uplift others who were facing similar obstacles.

Guided by empathy, I sought ways to aid fellow single parents who were grappling with challenges similar to those I had experienced. Recognizing that I couldn't single-handedly unravel all their complexities, I still understood that every small gesture of assistance held the potential to make a substantial impact on their lives. Refining my mental landscape became a cornerstone of this transformation. Purposefully, I nurtured a mindset oriented toward positivity and solutions, redirecting my energy from fixating on problems to envisioning ways to overcome them. I consciously refrained from vocalizing minor setbacks, recognizing that voicing negativity granted it power, both over myself and those who heard it. By stopping the cycle of negativity, I prevented bringing more of what I didn't want into my life.

By embracing gratitude and staying positive, a remarkable change happened. This shift in perspective led to a rapid influx of positivity, reshaping my reality and showing me how our outlook impacts our experiences.

Putting an End to Worry

On my journey, overcoming the relentless cycle of worry proved to be a significant milestone. The weight of my past experiences had ingrained in me an unhealthy habit of incessant worrying, turning my mind into a battlefield of anxiety with every potential outcome and unrealized obstacle. I found myself essentially being a walking ball of fear and stress. However, as I embraced the power of positive thinking, a revelation dawned upon me, exposing the futility of excessive worrying. This newfound perspective liberated me from the grip of anxiety, allowing me to navigate life with greater clarity, peace, and resilience.

Once a chaotic racetrack of thoughts darting in every conceivable direction, my mind underwent a transformation. It learned to hinge on the situation at hand, breaking free from the shackles of constant worry. No longer did I expend energy on fretting over every potential mistake; instead, I embraced living in the moment. When faced with unfavorable situations, I confronted them head-on, channeling my focus solely into finding solutions for each predicament. Remarkably, the decision to relinquish worry began to yield tangible effects, offering a sense of lightness and liberation from the stress that had tightly gripped me.

With determination, I directed my thoughts away from the endless spiral of worry, witnessing a remarkable transformation. The heavy burden that had weighed me down for so long, draining 90% of my emotional energy, began to lighten. As I embraced mindfulness techniques to combat worries, the power of choosing not to dwell on them became increasingly clear. Instead of fixating on negative outcomes, I deliberately shifted my focus to positive possibilities and took practical steps to address any concerns. Gradually, this deliberate change in mindset loosened worry's grip on my life, allowing me to reclaim my emotional well-being and concentrate on more productive endeavors. Here are the steps I took to conquer my goals and surpass my self-imposed limitations.

Taking ACTION

Understanding that bringing things to life requires more than mere wishes is crucial. While imagining and believing are vital, they serve as the blueprint for a grand structure, laying the groundwork but being insufficient on their own. True manifestation entails translating these thoughts and beliefs into action, as action forms the essential foundation upon which the envisioned reality must be constructed. Just as a magnificent building requires both a solid blueprint and a sturdy foundation, so does the process of manifesting demand a harmonious interplay of vision and action for transformative outcomes.

Manifestation isn't a magical shortcut; it's a dynamic interplay between your thoughts and your actions. Consider a scenario where your aspiration is to complete a marathon. While adding this goal to your vision board is a positive step, it's merely the spark. To turn this aspiration into reality, you must engage in deliberate planning and take actionable steps. The marathon won't unfold at your doorstep without your active involvement.

Your journey toward abundance relies on bridging the gap between thought and action. Your ability to translate your thoughts into tangible efforts holds the key. While dreaming is your starting point, it's the deliberate pursuit of those dreams through consistent action that turns the abstract into the concrete. The journey of manifestation doesn't conclude with mere contemplation; it reaches its climax as you steadfastly stride toward your objectives.

The Power of Writing:

Documenting your dreams and goals is a transformative practice that can have profound benefits for your personal growth and success. When you take the time to write down your aspirations, you give them a tangible presence in your life. This act of externalizing your thoughts not only clarifies what you want to achieve but also reinforces your commitment to pursuing those goals.

By putting your goals into writing, you create a clear roadmap for your subconscious mind to follow. Your written words serve as a constant reminder of your objectives, helping you stay focused and motivated. This process can also help you break down your goals into smaller, actionable steps, making them feel more achievable.

Moreover, documenting your dreams and goals allows you to track your progress over time. As you make strides toward your objectives, you can reflect on how far you've come and celebrate your accomplishments. Additionally, writing down your goals enables you to identify any obstacles or challenges you may encounter along the way, allowing you to develop strategies to overcome them.

In essence, the practice of documenting your dreams and goals empowers you to take ownership of your future. It transforms vague ideas into concrete plans and provides you with a framework for turning your aspirations into reality. Whether you're striving for personal growth, career advancement, or any other form of success, this simple yet powerful practice can be a game-changer on your journey toward fulfillment and achievement.

Crafting a Vision Board for Manifestation

When it comes to pursuing your dreams and aspirations, embracing the power of visualization and goal setting is key. Take the time to clearly define what you want to achieve and visualize yourself already living that reality. Create a vision board filled with images, words, and symbols that represent your goals and aspirations, and place it somewhere you'll see it every day. This will keep your goals at the forefront of your mind and help you stay focused and motivated.

Additionally, don't underestimate the importance of taking action. While visualization is powerful, it's equally important to take concrete steps toward your goals. Break down your goals into smaller, manageable tasks, and take consistent action toward achieving them. Celebrate your progress along the way, and don't be afraid to adjust your goals or approach as needed.

Stay open to opportunities and be willing to adapt to change. Life is full of unexpected twists and turns, and sometimes the path to your goals may not unfold exactly as you envisioned. Stay flexible, stay positive, and trust in your ability to overcome challenges and achieve success. Remember, every step you take brings you closer to realizing your dreams.

Keep in mind, this practice of visualization and goal setting may help accelerate your manifestation journey, bringing your desires to fruition more quickly.

The Art of Affirmation

In my experience, alongside visually mapping out your goals, speaking them aloud adds an extra layer of affirmation and strength to the manifestation process. Verbally expressing your aspirations engages another dimension of your awareness. When you vocalize your goals, you not only clarify and solidify them but also deepen their impact, embedding them more firmly into your belief system.

Speaking out loud acts as a transformative link, translating your thoughts into spoken words that bridge your inner desires with the outside world. By vocalizing your ambitions, you extend them beyond your mind, sending them out into the universe. This verbal manifestation creates a resonance that can shape your mindset, actions, and interactions, bringing them into harmony with the reality you aim to achieve.

I've found this method to be incredibly effective. When you speak your goals aloud, you're not just sharing them with others; you're also reinforcing them within yourself. The power of spoken words carries weight and commitment, motivating you to take action. In addition, discussing your goals with others can attract like-minded individuals, mentors, or collaborators who can offer valuable support, guidance, and connections along your journey.

Tapping into the Potential of Your Subconscious Mind

Engaging in the acts of writing, creating, and speaking serves as a focused and directed connection to your subconscious mind. Operating tirelessly behind the scenes, your subconscious processes information and actively seeks ways to transform your thoughts into reality. By consistently feeding it your aspirations and desires, you essentially program your subconscious to be a dedicated ally in the pursuit of your goals. Regardless of the scale or complexity of your dreams, big or small, simple or intricate, your subconscious mind becomes a powerful force working in tandem with you to turn them into tangible achievements.

When you take the time to jot down your dreams and delve into their intricacies, your brain initiates a transformative process. It begins to construct pathways and carve out routes, strategically working to bring your aspirations to life. Throughout this journey, you'll observe a remarkable alignment of ideas, individuals, and opportunities in your life. These newfound connections act as tools, elevating your thoughts to the next level. The synergy between your conscious efforts and the intricate workings of your subconscious mind becomes a catalyst for realizing the full potential of your dreams.

In my own exploration of the power of the mind, I found Ed Mylett's book, *The Power of One More*, to be particularly enlightening. It delves into how our desires shape our reality in intricate ways. For example, if you desire a blue van, you'll start noticing blue vans everywhere, even in places you hadn't noticed them before. This showcases the incredible ability of our brains to pick up on what's relevant to us. This heightened awareness then guides our focus, showing us how our thoughts manifest in our everyday experiences. As you align your thoughts and actions, important elements for reaching your goals become clearer. Your mind guides you on a path toward realizing your aspirations, turning desires into realities. This interaction between your intentions and your mind's workings helps bring your goals to life.

Manifesting your desires demands more than just hoping for the best; it requires your active involvement. It all begins with identifying what truly resonates with you, igniting the journey of manifestation. As you delve into your inner world, your mind acts as a guiding force, uncovering opportunities and clearing paths toward your aspirations. Yet, the true power lies in taking intentional steps based on these insights. Action becomes the vital link between envisioning and accomplishing, transforming dreams into tangible realities. This purposeful approach empowers you to actively shape your life's trajectory. Engaging deeply in this process can redefine your life, turning aspirations into lived experiences. Manifestation becomes a personal partnership between envisioning your dreams and taking proactive steps to bring them to fruition. To prevent feeling overwhelmed, focus on taking small, manageable steps—one at a time. Consistent progress, regardless of its scale, brings you closer to realizing your goals, leading to profound and positive transformations in your life.

Balancing Dreams and Reality

In my own experience, I've found that while imagining a better outcome is straightforward, the real challenge lies in turning those visions into reality. It's a common struggle we all face—knowing the solution but hesitating to act on it. Take, for example, the morning rush and perpetual tardiness. We know that waking up earlier is the solution, yet hitting the snooze button becomes a habit that's hard to break.

It's puzzling why we often hesitate to take action, especially when the answers seem clear. The tools to solve our problems are right there, but something holds us back from putting them into practice. It's like there's a barrier between our intentions and our actions. Habits persist because they provide a sense of comfort and familiarity, even if they're not serving us well in the long run.

Making positive changes requires consistent effort and discipline, which can be tough to maintain. The discomfort of change, coupled with the fear of failure or the unknown, creates resistance. It's easy to lose motivation when faced with obstacles, so it's crucial to find ways to stay committed.

One effective strategy is to set clear, achievable goals and create actionable plans to reach them. Having someone to hold you accountable can also make a big difference. And perhaps most importantly, cultivating self-awareness about what triggers your inaction and finding ways to motivate yourself can be incredibly powerful.

It's important to remember that simply acknowledging a problem isn't enough; it's the consistent actions we take afterward that truly drive change. And the good news is, even small adjustments can lead to significant transformations if we stick with them.

Coco Chanel's analogy of banging one's head against a wall, hoping for it to transform into a door, vividly encapsulates the sense of frustration and futility that often accompanies spending time in unproductive loops. For years, I found myself trapped in this cycle, tirelessly exerting effort and energy, yet seeing little to no progress. It was as if I were trying to force my way through a narrow rabbit hole, oblivious to the numerous open doors beckoning me toward new possibilities.

Despite my best efforts, I remained stuck in this pattern, grappling with the same challenges and obstacles time and time again. Each attempt to break free from the cycle only seemed to reinforce my feelings of frustration and disillusionment. I couldn't understand why my hard work wasn't yielding the results I desired, and I felt increasingly discouraged with each passing day.

It wasn't until I took a step back and reflected on Coco Chanel's analogy that I began to see the root of the problem. I realized that I had been approaching my goals with a narrow focus, constantly banging my head against the same proverbial wall in the hopes that it would somehow transform into an opening. I was so fixated on pushing through obstacles that I failed to see the alternative paths and opportunities that lay before me.

With this newfound insight, I began to adopt a more holistic approach to problem-solving. Instead of blindly persevering in the face of adversity, I started to explore other avenues and consider alternative solutions. I embraced the idea that progress isn't always linear and that sometimes, success lies in taking a step back and reassessing the situation from a different perspective.

As I shifted my mindset and embraced a more flexible and adaptive approach, I started to see tangible progress in various areas of my life. Doors that had previously been closed to me began to open, revealing new opportunities and possibilities that I had never considered before. It was a powerful reminder that sometimes, the key to success lies not in brute force or relentless determination, but in the willingness to explore new paths and embrace change.

In 2024, I embraced the mantra, "Are you willing to see it differently?" as my guiding phrase. This simple yet powerful question served as a spark for shifting my perspective and instigating necessary changes in my life. Continuously committed to growth and learning, I'm now able to remain open to new viewpoints and approaches.

Today, I no longer feel trapped in the cycle of banging my head against the wall. Instead, I approach challenges with a sense of curiosity and open-mindedness, knowing that each obstacle is an opportunity for growth and learning. And while the journey may still have its ups and downs, I take comfort in knowing that I am no longer confined to a narrow rabbit hole but free to explore the endless possibilities that lie beyond.

Navigating the journey of manifestation necessitates emotional mastery. While problems and setbacks are inevitable, your mindset transforms, viewing them not as insurmountable barriers but as minor bumps in the road. Managing your emotions becomes crucial. It's not about feigning a perfect life but addressing negative emotions constructively and promptly shifting to positive thoughts. Just as you change the TV channel to avoid an unpleasant show, you can switch your thought patterns. When negativity creeps in, change the mental channel—recall happy memories, connect with a friend, or focus on positive aspects.

This practice of "changing the channel" becomes a potent tool to break the downward spiral of negative thoughts. With consistent effort, your mind becomes adept at automatically shifting to positive perspectives over time. This shift empowers you to maintain emotional equilibrium and exhibit resilience in the face of challenges.

By embracing this mindset, you transition from forcing outcomes to allowing opportunities. Liberating yourself from the struggle of wall-banging, you confidently stride through the open doors that unfold on your journey toward growth and abundance.

The Significance of Emotional Well-being

Our emotions and perspectives wield substantial influence in shaping our experiences and overall state of well-being. When encountering someone who radiates positivity, finds silver linings in most situations, and uplifts those around them, we witness a person who is content and leading a fulfilling life. Conversely, an individual who is persistently negative, complaining about external circumstances, and exuding an aura of anger reflects someone ensnared in misery, unable to embrace the joys of life.

Remarkably, both these paths are outcomes of our thoughts and choices. If caught in a cycle of stress, worry, and fear, it becomes challenging to fully engage with life's richness and potential. To unlock greater fulfillment, cultivating feelings of joy and gratitude is essential.

Choosing a positive approach to life doesn't mean ignoring challenges or pretending perfection. Instead, it involves framing situations in a way that empowers you to navigate difficulties and setbacks more effectively. Maintaining a mindset focused on joy and gratitude lays the groundwork for growth, resilience, and an elevated sense of well-being.

Ultimately, the journey to a more abundant and satisfying life starts within. Your thoughts and emotional states profoundly impact your experiences. By consciously steering your thoughts toward positivity, gratitude, and joy, you not only enhance your own well-being but also exert a powerful and uplifting influence on the world around you.

Unveiling Your Purpose

Embarking on the journey to discover and embrace your sense of purpose is a transformative venture with the potential to influence every facet of your life. This process entails introspection, delving into your passions, values, strengths, and aspirations, weaving together the unique threads of your story.

At its core, your purpose becomes the driving force behind your actions and decisions. It instills a profound sense of meaning and fulfillment, fueling not only your ambitions but also creating a sense of flow in activities resonant with your core essence. Yet the path to uncovering your purpose is not always straightforward, often clouded by external expectations, societal norms, and material pursuits.

The journey of self-discovery begins with introspection, reflecting on your passions, interests, talents, and values. Identifying activities that make you lose track of time and bring genuine joy provides valuable clues to the heart of your purpose. Acknowledging and nurturing your strengths and uniqueness is also integral, guiding you toward roles and endeavors where you can shine and make a positive impact.

Exploring your passions and strengths helps you to identify patterns and themes that resonate with you, offering insights into the direction your purpose might take. Seeking inspiration from role models and mentors who are successfully aligned with their purpose provides additional guidance and perspectives.

Crucially, discovering your purpose is an ongoing process, a continuous journey of growth and exploration. Your purpose might evolve with new experiences, self-discovery, and adapting to changing circumstances. Embracing your purpose empowers you to live a deeply authentic and meaningful life, guiding choices, motivating actions, and infusing your days with purposeful direction. By aligning with your purpose, you contribute to your well-being and make a positive impact on the world around you.

The Power of Your WHY

Understanding and identifying your WHY is a potent force that shapes your pursuit of a dream future. Delving into your motivations establishes a robust foundation for your goals. When challenges arise, having a clear and compelling WHY provides the strength to persevere. In difficult times, your WHY becomes an anchor, a source of inspiration reminding you why you started and what you strive to achieve.

Discovering your own WHY is transformative. It shifts your perspective from drifting along to being guided by a purpose uniquely yours, bringing about remarkable changes. Beyond personal growth, understanding your WHY attracts opportunities and connections. As you align actions with your purpose, like-minded individuals enter your orbit, understanding your journey, sharing your values, and offering support.

The process of self-discovery and clarifying your WHY becomes a catalyst for personal growth. It uncovers your true passions and aspirations, attracting resources and knowledge relevant to your path. The newfound clarity seems to elicit a response from the universe, providing the tools needed to move forward on your purposeful journey.

Author Note:

I understand what you're thinking—finding your WHY can seem like an overwhelming task. Trust me, I've been there. When I first embarked on the journey of discovering my WHY, I was completely lost. While I could easily recite what others wanted for me, I had never taken the time to explore my own desires. So, when I sat down with a pen in hand, ready to write down my hopes and dreams, I found myself at a loss for words. It took some time for me to get comfortable with the process of writing and expressing my innermost thoughts. At first, I simply wrote about my day and my aspirations, grappling with self-doubt and the fear of judgment. However, despite my fears, I pushed through and started writing anyway. And you know what? I'm incredibly grateful that I did. Writing not only helped me uncover my WHY and my purpose, but it also empowered me to take action toward turning my dreams into reality.

In the upcoming segment, the focus will shift to the transformative journey that unfolds when one fully comprehends Manifestation, Gratitude, and Action. This powerful combination forms an equation that propels individuals toward extraordinary results. By properly incorporating these principles, you unlock the potential to sculpt your reality and attain what might initially appear implausible. The subsequent chapter delves into the profound impact that my newfound wisdom had on my life.

Boundary-less Life

After years of grappling with stagnation in my quest for progress, I finally mastered the integration of manifestation into my life. Armed with a constructive outlook, a sense of gratitude, and the commitment to challenging the person I was the day before, my life embarked on an unparalleled journey of growth!

Impactful Initiatives

Since its inception in 2017, Driving Single Parents Inc. has positively impacted numerous single-parent families, with the vehicles provided serving as tools to elevate their overall circumstances. Some have pursued higher education, secured better-paying jobs, and achieved the dream of homeownership. The vehicles signify more than transportation; they're symbols of hope and progress.

The profound impact is evident in the fact that four beneficiaries have assumed roles as board members, contributing their experiences and perspectives. Their engagement substantially contributes to our goal to empower single parents, allowing them to regain control over their lives.

The conception of this nonprofit was spontaneous, emerging over dinner one evening. By translating the idea into action, I paved the way for Driving Single Parents Inc. to come to life. This underscores the truth that having all the answers is not a prerequisite; transforming thoughts and aspirations into action is the key to discovering their potential. Even if an idea doesn't pan out, failure is an opportunity for growth. As Thomas Edison said, "I didn't fail, I just found 10,000 ways that didn't work." The key is to keep going, driven by your clear vision. Taking that step matters, and things often fall into place in surprising ways.

Personal, Professional, and Relationship Transformation

Before mastering emotional well-being and the art of manifestation, I found myself consistently entangled in unhealthy relationships, playing the role of a "fixer" who ignored warning signs and issues. This pattern was evident in all my past relationships. It wasn't until a journey of self-discovery that I confronted this hurdle and uncovered its root cause, prompting a profound shift in my perspective on friendships and relationships.

With positivity, love, and stability taking root, my life underwent a remarkable evolution. A new work opportunity materialized, placing me in an entirely different setting where growth and prospects were abundant. Bolstered by newfound self-assurance and belief, my career surged forward. Reflecting on the past 16 years, multiple career advancements had come my way, only for me to decline them due to a lack of confidence and self-imposed limitations. Yet, as I mastered the principles of manifestation and self-empowerment, I overcame these barriers and embraced the avenues of growth that had long been within reach.

The transformation I experienced wasn't confined to my professional endeavors; it permeated deeply into my personal life and the dynamics of my relationships. What became clear to me was that nurturing personal growth and prioritizing emotional well-being, coupled with a readiness to embrace change, could act as a catalyst for profound transformations across all spheres of life. Through recognizing and confronting my own limitations, I discovered the potential to unlock doors that were once obscured by layers of self-doubt. This journey serves as a testament to the extraordinary power of self-discovery and intentional evolution.

Despite achieving numerous milestones, one formidable fear persisted, demanding to be addressed head-on. Throughout my life's journey, I had grappled with feeling like an outsider, often plagued by a persistent self-critical mindset. The mere thought of drawing attention to myself filled me with a sense of dread, stemming from a deep-rooted fear of potential ridicule. During my formative years, I found myself meticulously rehearsing every word before speaking and obsessively analyzing every question before daring to voice it aloud. This fear had been a constant presence, casting a shadow over my interactions and holding me back from fully expressing myself.

Upon establishing Driving Single Parents, a significant facet of my role involved giving interviews and raising awareness about our impactful work. However, persistent apprehension and fear of public speaking held me captive. Recognizing the need to break free from this hindrance, I resolved to overcome this seemingly irrational fear, adding the aspiration to my vision board. I started writing about confidently speaking on podcasts, public platforms, and interviews, determined to cast aside fear and self-doubt.

In due course, I began responding affirmatively to every interview request, even though the prospect of public speaking left me trembling. This marked the initiation of my journey to dismantle self-doubt. With relentless practice and an ever-increasing number of interviews, I mustered the courage to confront my fear head-on. Gradually the fear receded as I found myself becoming more proficient in the art of public speaking.

The transformation was a result of consistent effort and determination to defy my insecurities. While the fear didn't vanish entirely, I learned to navigate it with grace and resilience. This journey serves as a testament to the potency of visualization, persistence, and pushing through discomfort. Overcoming self-doubt requires acknowledging its presence and committing to challenging it, step by step.

Surpassing the Boundaries of Belief

The notion of becoming an author seemed unattainable to me, and I dismissed it as absurd when it first crossed my mind. Convinced it was an impossible feat, I believed I lacked the intelligence and feared negative judgments from those close to me. Being a struggling single mother, I confined myself to flying under the radar, focusing on day-to-day survival and creating a better life for my daughters. The idea of becoming a published author was unequivocally on my "impossible" list.

Fast forward about five years, and I found myself co-authoring my first book, *Shattering the Stigma of Single Motherhood*, stepping into the realm of published authors. Looking back, I realized I could have achieved this much earlier had I embraced self-belief, documented my aspirations, and translated my thoughts into action. This story mirrors the experiences of many individuals who sideline their dreams, deeming them unrealistic or fearing external judgment, ultimately abandoning them before encountering failure. I, too, followed this pattern for much of my life.

It wasn't until I decided to shed concern for others' opinions, practice gratitude for what I had, believe in my capabilities, and solely compete with my past self that my life began to transform. This shift in mindset allowed my life to take form in unexpected ways. I hadn't realized the extent to which I had been limiting my own potential.

The takeaway from my journey is that we often underestimate our abilities and allow external opinions to hinder our progress. Embracing self-belief, gratitude, and a growth-oriented mindset can be immensely empowering. Disregarding external judgment and focusing on personal growth and progress enables us to surpass our own expectations and truly live up to our potential. My experience is a reminder that we are often the main obstacle standing in our own way, and overcoming this hurdle can lead to profound transformation.

Embracing Fear: A Path to Achievement

I embraced my fear and co-authored that book, eventually becoming an Amazon International Best-Selling Author. The overwhelming sense of accomplishment stemmed from pushing through my fear. Reflecting on the experience, I couldn't help but acknowledge how easily I could have stayed in my comfort zone, allowing that opportunity to slip away. But this time, I seized the moment, felt genuine pride in my achievement, and opened up a world of incredible people—a supportive community valuing collaboration over competition. The blend of pride, joy, and accomplishment, without any regret, is etched into my memory.

Following the success of *Shattering the Stigma of Single Motherhood*, I had opportunities to co-author multiple books, yet none resonated until I heard the title of a forthcoming book set to be released in the spring of 2023. At that moment, I knew I had found my next book project.

Accepting the invitation to co-author the anthology *Overcoming Self-Sabotage*, I confronted my fear once again, knowing that my story, particularly the challenging parts, could resonate with and assist others. Between the nonprofit and the release of the two books I co-authored, I've realized that sharing struggles illuminates a path for many to recognize that their past doesn't dictate their identity. Regardless of origins in poverty, experiences of domestic violence, single parenthood, or growing up in a single-parent household, we all have aspects of our lives that weren't ideal. What truly matters is how we transform those experiences into purpose.

Understanding this, I've come to realize that our past doesn't define us. We all hold the power to decide where our stories lead. The choices we make either propel us into the potential of our purpose or hold us back. This choice is entirely ours. The power to shatter self-limiting beliefs and propel ourselves to the next level resides within us. Recognizing this truth and acting on it is the key to achieving our loftiest aspirations.

At the close of 2022, after completing my first book project, *Shattering the Stigma of Single Motherhood*, and committing to being a co-author on the second book, *Overcoming Self-Sabotage*, a surge of confidence filled me. Contemplating what more I could achieve, I built a brand-new website and the idea of starting a business crossed my mind. I decided to register it as an LLC, making it the parent company for future ventures. Uncertain about the content of the website, I trusted my intuition to go for it, building it over time and adding services gradually.

My journey took another unexpected turn when I was presented with the possibility to host my own TV show.

Initially hesitant due to lingering fears of public speaking and the perceived absurdity of hosting a show with no prior experience, I rejected the idea at first. However, in January 2023, a spark of curiosity ignited within me, leading me to ponder, "What if?"

With this newfound sense of intrigue, I delved into the idea. Was it feasible for me to embark on a career as a TV show host? Did I truly want to pursue this path? Through consistent journaling and introspection, clarity gradually surfaced. It was during a dinner outing at my favorite steakhouse with my husband that the concept of *Little Give with Cindy* solidified in my mind.

Inspired by the inquiries about the driving force behind establishing Driving Single Parents, I recognized the need to showcase regular people taking impactful actions. The journey took a significant leap forward in the spring of 2023 when I assumed the role of host for the *Little Give* TV show, airing in 136 countries and dedicated to highlighting ordinary people doing extraordinary things to help others and shining a spotlight on various nonprofits worldwide.

In 2023, just on the cusp of my debut episode of *Little Give*, fate intervened once again, altering the course of my life in a split second. As I made my way to work, the routine walk from the parking garage to the elevator turned into an ordeal when a massive truck careened around the corner, colliding with me. The impact knocked me out of my shoes and I was halfway beneath the truck; the world seemed to stop as the driver realized the gravity of what had happened.

Though I only had minor cuts and bruises, the incident etched itself into the recesses of my mind, leaving me grappling with the fragility of life and the profound impact of my absence on my loved ones, especially my children and grandchildren. It was a wake-up call, forcing me to confront the question of my legacy—had I truly lived to my fullest potential, or had I been playing it safe all along?

In the wake of this near-death experience, I found myself propelled into a whirlwind of introspection and soul-searching. I made a solemn vow to seize every moment, to cherish my family with newfound appreciation, and to live unapologetically. The incident shattered any illusions of invincibility, driving home the realization that life is fleeting and precious.

Hosting the show has connected me with profoundly inspirational individuals globally, reaffirming the decision to embrace this opportunity. I've gained knowledge from guests tirelessly working to improve the world, encouraging others to give a little more every day.

The two questions that steer the show—"Can you give the audience an example of a little thing they can do in their community that might be a little give on their end but might make a big impact?" and "Can you share an example of a time in your life when someone did something little for you that may have been a little give on their end but made a big impact to you and in your life?"—are deeply personal reminders of the power of small gestures. Guests open up about their own experiences, highlighting how kindness creates ripples of positivity. This impact has expanded beyond the TV show, leading to the creation of a podcast spin-off called *Little Give—Podcast*, which shares the show's meaningful content with a wider audience.

Determined to banish self-doubt and take charge of my destiny, I sought solace in the company of like-minded individuals who shared my passion for service and authenticity. It was a profound shift—a liberation from the shackles of conformity and people-pleasing that had held me captive for so long. Embracing my newfound agency as the CEO of my own life, I embarked on a journey of self-discovery and empowerment, finding peace and fulfillment in embracing my truest self.

Fueled by a burning desire to pay forward the gift of survival, I continued to pursue my love for life and confidence coaching, eager to guide others on their path to self-realization and fulfillment. This calling, coupled with the three books I authored, became the cornerstone of CF Views LLC—a beacon of hope and transformation for those seeking to break free from the chains of self-doubt and live authentically.

CF Views LLC provides tailored coaching services focused on enhancing life and confidence, reflecting a strong commitment to empowering individuals in their pursuit of success and fulfillment. Integrating my books into the business model underscores our mission to offer both inspiration and actionable guidance for manifestation and conscious change. It's been an exciting ride, resonating deeply with my passions and aspirations to make a meaningful impact.

My latest endeavor involves the launch of my own magazine titled *FORCE: A Force to be Reckoned With*. With this publication, my goal is to showcase individuals who embody strength and influence in various aspects of their lives. *FORCE* magazine will serve as a source of inspiration, providing valuable information and empowering stories. Its pages will be filled with positive messages and insights into the ripple effect of kindness. Through this platform, I aim to uplift readers and motivate them to make a positive impact in their own lives and communities.

What truly sets this entrepreneurial venture apart is the seamless fusion of ambition, action, and fulfillment. Every step in building this business feels like a natural progression, driven by a genuine desire to create positive change. The alignment between my personal aspirations and the business's mission has turned it into a purpose-driven endeavor, where the joy derived from every aspect of our work serves as fuel for ongoing growth and impact.

Through CF Views LLC, I've not only turned my own dreams into reality but have also created a platform to offer meaningful support to others. The business stands as proof of the transformative power of aligning passions with tangible endeavors, illustrating how purposeful entrepreneurship can drive positive change in both individual lives and the broader community.

Sharing my personal journey of ups and downs, I aim to underscore the profound impact that manifestation can have on life. From battling insecurities to becoming the Founder/CEO of Driving Single Parents Inc., a three-time International Best-Selling Author, Business Owner, Founder of *FORCE* Magazine, Life and Confidence Coach, Entrepreneur, Speaker, and Podcaster, to hosting the *Little Give* TV show—I've crafted a multifaceted and fulfilling life. This journey from humble beginnings to significant achievements serves as proof that manifestation is a catalyst for change. In the next chapter, I'll offer additional guidance on integrating these principles into your life and embarking on a path toward abundance and self-discovery.

FOUNDATION OF GRATITUDE

How to apply this to your life:

To begin your journey, lay the groundwork by embracing each day with gratitude. Initially challenging for me, especially during my manifestation journey, I shifted my focus from lacking to appreciating what I already possessed. Awakening each morning, I consciously acknowledged gratitude for the smallest things before stepping out of bed. I found solace in sunlight, the aroma of morning coffee, or the joy of a new day. Three minutes each day dedicated to my gratitude journal further solidified this practice.

Expressing gratitude for both extraordinary and mundane aspects marked a crucial juncture in manifesting abundance. It reminded me of the blessings present—a supportive friend network, good health, the privilege of sunrise, and family love. This foundation became a cornerstone for manifesting positivity, serving as a daily reminder that, amid challenges, beauty, kindness, and opportunity abound. Acknowledging and appreciating these aspects became a powerful catalyst, setting the stage for more blessings and opportunities in my life.

ELIMINATE NEGATIVITY

In the pursuit of a positive and abundant life, it is imperative to eliminate negativity from your thoughts and expressions. The act of spreading negativity serves no purpose; rather, it perpetuates a cycle that fosters more negativity, frustration, and anger without contributing to any productive outcome.

Dwelling on unpleasant situations doesn't alter them; instead, it intensifies the impact of negativity. Both thinking and vocalizing negative thoughts can lead to a self-fulfilling prophecy, generating a detrimental cycle with no constructive results.

While it is beyond our control to dictate the actions of others, we have the power to manage our own reactions and behaviors. A valuable guideline in this journey is to refrain from voicing thoughts that don't contribute positively to ourselves or others. My grandmother imparted a timeless principle that continues to resonate: "If you don't have something nice to say, don't say anything at all." This sage advice serves as a reminder to choose our words wisely, opting for positivity instead of inadvertently contributing to a cycle of negativity.

By adhering to this principle, you take a proactive step in shaping a positive environment around you. It reinforces the idea that positivity breeds positivity, creating a space where constructive thoughts and actions can flourish. This commitment to eliminating negativity becomes an integral part of your manifestation journey, fostering an atmosphere that encourages growth, abundance, and lasting positivity.

ABANDON JUDGMENT

Navigating our intricate world, each person carries a tapestry of experiences, struggles, and triumphs that often remain concealed from external view. Despite our interactions, it's crucial to recognize that we lack access to the full spectrum of others' lives and emotions. This realization serves as a crucial reminder to abstain from judgment, acknowledging that appearances can be deceiving.

When we engage in judgment or criticism, we run the risk of oversimplifying the complexity of someone else's journey. Our perceptions can be clouded by personal biases, insecurities, and a limited understanding of their circumstances. As the age-old saying advises, "Don't judge a book by its cover." The same principle applies to individuals.

Choosing to withhold judgment contributes to fostering a culture of empathy and understanding. This not only benefits others but also profoundly impacts our own well-being. Releasing the impulse to criticize or compare ourselves to others lifts the unnecessary burden of negativity. The mental space once consumed by judgment becomes available for more productive and fulfilling thoughts.

In essence, breaking free from the habit of judgment allows

us to appreciate the beauty in diversity and the richness of each individual's unique story. It serves as a reminder that everyone is grappling with their own battles and striving for their personal versions of success. Embracing compassion and refraining from judgment cultivates a more harmonious and positive existence, benefiting both ourselves and those around us.

GIVE GRACE

As emphasized earlier, we rarely grasp the full extent of someone else's day. Instances of road rage from fellow drivers or encounters with irritable employees at checkout counters are experiences we've all encountered. It's crucial to extend grace to these individuals, acknowledging that their frustration likely originates from circumstances unrelated to your specific interaction. Be assured that the source of their agitation is unlikely to be you, as there's probably an external factor causing their stress and anger. Instead of allowing negativity to spread, choose to remain understanding. Avoid dwelling on the negative encounter and discussing it with others. Refrain from amplifying negativity; always give others the benefit of the doubt.

Remember, your reaction is the sole aspect you can control. By responding without negativity, you contribute to creating a more positive atmosphere for all involved. Demonstrating empathy and choosing to be gracious generates a ripple effect that fosters a more harmonious environment.

When it comes to extending grace, the most important person to offer it to is yourself. I've learned firsthand that we can be our own toughest critics. Whenever I start feeling overwhelmed by self-criticism or doubt, I remind myself not to engage in harsh inner dialogues. Instead, I consciously choose to give myself grace. I take a moment to reflect on what I can control and focus on taking positive action where necessary. I've realized the importance of not dwelling on the past or things beyond my control—it only drains my energy. So, I've learned to be patient with myself and actively seek ways to change the channel in my mind when negative thoughts arise. And remember, you have the power, too. After all, you can choose what narrative plays in your head, and you deserve to make it a positive one.

Here's a Pro Tip: Transform Your Mindset

I've found that allowing negative thoughts to linger only feeds into a cycle of negativity, clouding my perspective and impacting not only myself but also those I care about. The emotions stirred by these thoughts serve no purpose other than to drag me down. But I've come to realize that I possess the power to change the narrative. When I recognize a negative thought pattern creeping in, I consciously choose to pivot toward a more positive and constructive mindset.

By redirecting my thoughts and emotions, I not only lift my own spirits but also create a ripple effect of positivity in my interactions with others. It's a journey of self-discovery and growth, where I'm learning to take ownership of my mindset and shape it into one that fosters fulfillment and productivity. Embracing this mindset shift has empowered me to navigate life's challenges with resilience and optimism, paving the way for a brighter and more fulfilling path ahead.

SHIFTING YOUR MINDSET: A GUIDE

The concept of mindset is pervasive, but affecting a true shift requires conscious effort. It's not a simple task, and it demands dedicated practice. So, how do you genuinely transform your mindset? Let me explain: The most potent method involves training your brain to perceive the positive aspects of life, actively steering away from negative thoughts and emotions.

Initially, this process will demand manual intervention; it won't come easily. Yet, as you consistently adopt the habit of cultivating positive thoughts regardless of circumstances, you'll find yourself gaining control over your emotions and reactions. It's a challenging but immensely rewarding practice. As your mindset evolves, changes in the way others communicate with you and the way you're treated will become evident. Suddenly, you'll recognize that people are generally kind and generous. The shift is profound: Where once you were fixated on negativity, your mind will now naturally gravitate toward positivity. This newly cultivated positive mindset will reveal the good in situations that previously went unnoticed. In time, the positive aspects of life will present themselves more frequently, shaping a more uplifting and harmonious existence.

Pro Tip: Break the Negative Cycle.

Ultimately, the key is to be mindful of your thoughts and actively replace negative ones with positive alternatives. Whether you choose to employ the rubber band method or explore other strategies, the overarching goal remains unchanged: to train your brain to embrace positivity and guide your mindset toward a more fulfilling and optimistic outlook on life.

Don't get me wrong—I'm not here to coach you into having your head in the clouds or to encourage you to ignore legitimate issues in your life. What I'm suggesting is taking a moment to pause and assess whether the negative thoughts you're experiencing are within your control to change, or if they're merely worries about the past or about uncertain outcomes.

For instance, if you rush out of the house in the morning only to realize later that you left your flat iron plugged in and on the counter, that's a tangible problem that requires immediate action. However, if you find yourself fretting over a comment you or someone else made two days ago, it's time to shift your focus to the positive. No amount of worrying will alter the past, so why waste precious energy dwelling on it?

Always take a second to ask yourself: Am I investing my time and energy into contemplating a negative situation that I have the power to change, or am I simply spinning my wheels over something beyond my control? If there's nothing you can do to alter the outcome, it's time to kick those negative thoughts to the curb. Change the channel in your mind to something that brings you joy and fulfillment instead. Your mental well-being deserves that much.

ELIMINATING SELF-DOUBT

I've battled self-doubt and self-sabotage for as long as I can remember. Growing up in a family where resources were scarce, I often found myself feeling inadequate and questioning my worth. It seemed like there was always something holding me back, something inside me that just wasn't good enough. This constant struggle with my own confidence made me hesitant to pursue my dreams or take risks in life.

But I've come to realize that overcoming self-sabotage starts with recognizing your own value and embracing your unique strengths. Despite what those nagging doubts may tell you, you possess a set of abilities and talents that are entirely your own. You are deserving of success and happiness, and there's no limit to what you can achieve when you believe in yourself.

Once I started to shift my perspective and truly believe in my own potential, I noticed a remarkable change in how I approached life. Suddenly, challenges didn't seem so insurmountable, and opportunities didn't feel so out of reach. I began to understand the wisdom in Warren Buffett's words: "The most important investment you can make is in yourself." By investing in your own self-belief and casting aside those doubts, you create a foundation for growth and achievement that knows no bounds.

Pro Tip: Tune in to Your Self-Talk

When challenges emerge, a valuable practice is to attentively listen to your own reactions. Pay close attention to the words you use, especially when negativity creeps in. Observe instances in which you use phrases like "I can't," "I won't," "but," "I could if," and "when."

This heightened self-awareness serves as the initial step toward authentic manifestation. Rewiring your thought patterns and training your brain requires meticulous attention to the language you use. By consciously reshaping your self-talk, you lay the groundwork for transforming your beliefs and ultimately paving the way to manifesting your aspirations. Incorporate and use the following steps as a helpful guide during your journey of manifestation. By integrating these principles into your approach, you can navigate the path toward manifesting your desires with greater clarity and purpose.

Step 1: Get Writing

Kickstart your journey toward abundance with a simple yet powerful step—writing. This foundational practice sets your intentions in motion, even if your initial attempts feel a bit scattered or unclear. Dedicate just six minutes each day to jotting down your aspirations, allowing your thoughts to flow freely. Break it down into three-minute sessions, one in the morning and another before bedtime, to frame your reflections for the day.

Step 2: Uncover Your WHY

Dig deeper into your goals by discovering your WHY. This intrinsic motivation becomes your guiding light, especially during tough times. If your dreams extend beyond yourself—to benefiting loved ones or the community—this WHY becomes your unwavering commitment, helping you persevere through challenges.

Step 3: Picture Your Goals

Visualization is a potent tool in bringing your dreams to life. Picture your goals vividly, whether it's starting a business or achieving personal milestones. Translate these mental images onto paper, outlining essential components of your vision. Visualization and writing ground your aspirations in reality, guiding your thoughts toward actionable plans.

Step 4: Connect with Like-Minded People

Building a supportive network is crucial. Surround yourself with individuals who share your ambitions or have achieved similar goals. Engaging with like-minded people offers valuable guidance, motivation, and a sense of belonging, creating a supportive community to fuel your journey.

Step 5: Create a Vision Board

Take your visualization to the next level by creating a vision board. Compile images and words that resonate deeply with your desired accomplishments. Engage with your vision board daily, immersing yourself in the emotions associated with achieving your goals.

Step 6: Cultivate Positive Emotions

Visualize the joy and satisfaction of realizing your dreams. By immersing yourself in these positive emotions, you strengthen your connection to your goals and stay motivated to overcome obstacles.

Step 7: Stay Consistent

Consistently revisit your goals, track your progress, and refine your plans. Trust the process, maintain a consistent rhythm of action, and stay committed to your journey.

Step 8: Control Your Thoughts

Choose positivity to invite positive experiences into your life. Redirect your thoughts toward gratitude, possibility, and success, rewiring your brain to default to a positive mindset.

Step 9: Respond Mindfully

Practice mindful responses over knee-jerk reactions, preserving inner peace and fostering understanding in challenging situations.

Step 10: Curate Your Inner Circle

Surround yourself with individuals who support your aspirations and uplift your spirit. Spend time with those who inspire and challenge you to grow.

By embracing these expanded steps, you're embarking on a comprehensive journey toward manifesting abundance. Align your thoughts, emotions, and actions with your goals, creating powerful momentum toward your desired future. With each step, you actively design a life reflecting your true potential and abundance.

Navigating Life's Ebb and Flow

Recognizing that a life centered on manifestation isn't shielded from life's ups and downs is essential. Like everyone else, I encounter challenges, tough days, and negative thoughts. The difference lies in my response. When faced with adversity, I view it as an opportunity for growth, learning, and the pursuit of my next goal. This journey isn't always smooth sailing; it's a continuous process of development and evolution. And that's okay—because setbacks only add depth to my story.

As you embark on your journey to manifest a life without limits, understand that it's not about perfection or being immune to challenges. It's about persistence, determination, and the willingness to press forward in the face of obstacles. As Krystalore Crews wisely said, "The Work Works when you do the Work." Your efforts, actions, and mindset will shape the life you're building. Stay committed and unwavering in the face of setbacks, and eventually, you'll look back and appreciate the significant progress you've made. In those moments, you'll realize that your transformation is a testament to your dedication and the endless potential within you.

IN CONCLUSION

Let me emphasize once again: Stop comparing yourself to others! In today's digital age, particularly with the prevalence of social media, it's effortless to get caught up in the facade of others' seemingly flawless lives. Yet, rest assured, nobody has everything figured out, and countless individuals out there yearn to be in your shoes. It's imperative for us all to abandon the notion of perfection and begin acknowledging the inherent power within ourselves. Believe it or not, that power resides within you, waiting to be unleashed and shared with the world. Each of us possesses unique talents and gifts, so let's discard the habit of comparison and competition, and instead, focus on nurturing our individual strengths and potential.

I used to spend my earlier years constantly pushing to get ahead, but now that I've realized the power within me, I've stepped into my purpose, and now it propels me forward. Find what you love and do more of that! Doing so will guarantee your happiness and your ability to overcome any circumstance that presents itself. Look inward, go "beyond the smile," and you'll discover your highest self.

The journey to manifesting a life beyond limits is profound and transformative. By following the steps outlined in this guide, you can tap into your inner potential and shape a reality aligned with your dreams. Remember, it all starts with writing down your hopes and dreams, setting clear goals, and discovering your WHY for motivation.

Visualization and surrounding yourself with like-minded individuals can amplify your efforts, while consistent action and a positive mindset are essential for bringing your dreams to life. Embrace gratitude, eliminate negativity, and discard self-doubt to propel yourself forward. You are the creator of your reality, and the power of your thoughts and actions is immense.

Through real-life stories and experiences, we've witnessed how these principles work wonders in transforming lives. While the journey may pose challenges, by remaining persistent, adaptable, and open to learning, you can overcome obstacles and continue on the path of growth and abundance.

Thank you for joining me on this journey of self-discovery and empowerment. Remember, the power within you can manifest a life beyond limits. Keep believing in yourself, taking action, and nurturing a positive mindset. Your dreams are waiting to be realized—go out there and make them a reality! If you're interested in learning more about my endeavors or connecting, please feel free to visit the following websites or reach out via email.

Contact Information:

Email: If you have any inquiries or wish to connect, feel free to reach out directly at info@mail.cfviews.com

Websites:

Explore more about our nonprofit organization and its mission to support single parents by visiting DrivingSingleParents.org (https://www.drivingsingleparents.org/).

Little Give TV Show: Discover inspiring stories of ordinary people making extraordinary contributions on the *Little Give* TV show (https://www.littlegive.com/).

Little Give Podcast: Prefer podcasts? Listen to the Little Give podcast on major streaming platforms or directly on LittleGive.com (https://cfviews.com/little-give-podcast).

Life & Confidence Coaching, *FORCE* Magazine, Books: For information on life and confidence coaching, *FORCE* Magazine, and books authored by me, please visit CFViews.com (https://www.cfviews.com/).

Get featured in *FORCE* Magazine: CFViews.com
https://cfviews.com/%E2%80%9Cforce%E2%80%9D-magazine

About the Author

I'm Cindy Witteman, based in San Antonio, Texas. I'm involved in various roles: I'm a Business Owner and a 3x International Best-Selling Author. Furthermore, I'm humbled to have received the 2023 International Impact Book Award. I also lead as the Host of both the "Little Give" TV Show and the "Is Manifesting Bullshit Podcast" and am the Founder/CEO of FORCE Magazine. Alongside these roles, I've been honored with the 2023 Trailblazer Award. I also serve as an Entrepreneur, Action Mastery Coach, Speaker, and Beekeeper. In 2017, I established Driving Single Parents Inc., a non-profit dedicated to assisting single parents in reclaiming their independence. With a blended family consisting of six kids, one grandson, and two granddaughters, family time is invaluable to me, and I'm passionate about travel. Through Driving Single Parents Inc., I've positively impacted countless lives by providing reliable vehicles to single-parent families, empowering them to surmount challenges and achieve success.

Founder & CEO of Driving Single Parents, Inc., Host of Little Give TV Show & Owner of CFViews LLC

https://www.linkedin.com/in/cindy-witteman-a48851253
https://www.facebook.com/cindy.witt.902
https://www.instagram.com/cindy.witteman/
www.DrivingSingleParents.org
www.LittleGive.com
www.CFViews.com

FORCE Magazine

Are you a FORCE to be reckoned with? Get featured in FORCE Magazine: https://sites.cfviews.com/force-magazine

Join us in supporting single parents by visiting
DrivingSingleParents.org

a 501(c)3 non-profit dedicated to providing vehicles to deserving single-parent families at NO cost to them.

Little Give TV Show

Visit LittleGive.com to watch ordinary people doing extraordinary things to help others. Want to be a guest on the show?

Schedule a pre-show interview here:
https://link.brandbuilderai.com/widget/bookings/littlegive

CF Views LLC

Explore CFViews.com for advertising opportunities, life-confidence coaching, and to learn more about FORCE Magazine.

Are you ready to share your story or become a featured author or speaker? Visit the website to get involved.

Is Manifesting Bullshit Podcast

Tune in to the "Is Manifesting Bullshit?" podcast on [Apple Podcasts] (https://podcasts.apple.com/us/podcast/is-manifesting-b-t/id1706597978) for insightful discussions on the power of manifesting.

FREE Mastermind Group

Join our FREE Mastermind Group on Facebook for support and inspiration:
https://www.facebook.com/groups/866921888545418/?ref=share&mibextid=K35XfP

Let's make a positive impact together!

www.ingramcontent.com/pod-product-compliance
Lightning Source LLC
Chambersburg PA
CBHW072116050526
44107CB00098BA/266